Getting Stitches
Poems by Rudy Francisco

Dedication

I dedicate this collection of poems to the first writer I knew,
my brother Lasalle Francisco

Contents

Page

Skeleton

When there is no soul
left in this body,
put my skeleton on a string
give the sunlight permission
to play freeze tag with my bones.
I've always wanted to be a wind chime

A Few Things I believe

Sour Apple flavored
anything is delicious,
Orange Juice tastes
better with pulp
and Cinnabon
is made by angels.
I like Arizona Icea Tea,
but 24 ounces of anything
for 99 cents is definitely poison.

I believe masculinity is a wet fish
that most men are just trying to hold onto
and smiling before a fight
is the quickest way to make
your opponent nervous.

I believe music is easier
to digest than medicine,
a good song can turn
any room into a church
and Whitney Houston's voice
is all the proof I need
to know God exists.

A Letter to the Apocalypse

Your name
has become synonymous
with free iPads, reparations
and a whole bunch of
other things that wont
be happen anytime soon.

You've become the
laughing-stock of all disasters.
I imagine hurricanes make fun of you.
I bet your girlfriend is cheating
on you with a snowstorm.
Donald Trump says he wants
to see your birth certificate.
And if you won a Grammy,
Kanye West would interrupt you.

Apocalypse,
The people are laughing.
They think you're just
another prank call from God,
a punch line in Revelations.
They act like you're not the rapture,
like you're not the last chapter of the bible,
like you're not wrath, smoke and lightning.
Tell these people you're the Armageddon,
a clenched fist waiting for a reason,
a hammer in the right hand
of Divine Intervention.
They have clearly forgotten
that you are hellfire and brimstone.
They snicker when you're
mentioned in conversation,

they put "lol" next to your name on twitter.
These people don't respect you.

I'm not saying you should've ended the world,
but you could've at least knocked down a tree.
Let them know you mean business.

The Body

Dear eyes,
There are things I don't tell you.
We both know that you are
terrible at keeping secrets.

Dear brain,
You're a good listener
but you give horrible
relationship advice.

Dear heart,
I trust you
don't let me down.

Dear legs,
Walking is easy
now pick a destination

Dear feet,
Some days, you are all
 I have left to stand on

Dear hands,
I know you love writing poetry
but you can't bring
a metaphor to a fistfight

Dear fists,
When words fail
sometimes, I let you
handle my problems

Dear voice,
You have their attention
say something worth remembering.
I'm counting on you

Definitions

Envy
is when someone walks around with a
pocket full of "that should've been me."

Insecure
is when you turn up the volume
on all the wrong voices.

Hate
is what happens when you put
a shotgun to the face of understanding
and it cowers in the corner.

Courage
is ripping your heart from your chest
and saying "here…hold on to this for me."

Truth
 is everything you tell yourself
when you realize you are the
only one still paying attention.

Self
is whoever you become
when the door is locked.

Trust
is jumping into someone's arms
and knowing you won't have to
pick yourself up when it's over.

Love
is a tablespoon full of hemlock

I've been dying to try.

Faith
is doing what you love for a living
and watching the bills pay themselves.

Failure
is when you talk yourself out of
becoming something amazing.

Victory
is standing in front the
school bully with no intention to
back down and a fist full of irony.

Success
is explaining to your mother
exactly what you do for a living
without feeling ashamed.
It's falling asleep at 2 am,
waking up at 4 am and
going to work with excitement
stitched into the fabric of your smile.

Success
is a thank you letter from kid
who lives in a city you've
never even been to.
It's breaking up a fight
between a person and
everything that has told them
they will never be more than what they are.

When I was 14

my friend Adam stole a
dictionary from his English class.
He brought it home
and we set it on fire.
Since then,
I've been defining things for myself

Like Every Other Man

When she says,
you are like every other man
that she's every met,
her words will shift into
an angry hive of winged insults.
They will sting you in places
calamine lotion won't heal.
They will build a nest in the
medicine cabinet of your throat.
You feel them whenever you speak.

On this day,
your pride will have PTSD.
The citizenship of your
smile will get revoked.
It'll hide inside of your face
like it's afraid of being deported.
Her name will gyrate
in your stomach 24 hours
before a storm hits your city.
Your heart will become
a dusty piano.
she will play you
when no one is looking,
now you understand why
it's called an organ.

When she looks at the
clearance rack of items in her life
and tries to put you on a hanger
next to men with amateur stitching,

she is clearly forgetting
the mountains you've
placed in wheel-barrels,
simply because she
asked them to be moved.

Remind her that your
collar still tastes like salt
from all the oceans
she has cried into your shoulder.

Show her the bags
underneath your eyes
from all the nights
you've spent listening to her
talk about crippled relationships.

Make her look at your hands.
Let her see the leftover super glue
from the day her self-esteem
turned into a model
airplane with no instructions.

Ask her,
If you are so much
like these other men
why are you the
only one still here?

I thought you only dated white girls?

With surprise in
the cellar of her voice
and a residue of judgment
lingering on the
stained glass window of her tone.
In an octave higher than normal.
She says to me,
"You like black women?
I thought you
only dated white girls."

This a prison that men
like me find familiar.
A place where
we leave a toothbrush
because we sleep here so often.

My response was this:

Similar to all black men,
I have a mother.
Her name Simeona Francisco.
Her voice is the only pillow
I've ever been able to sleep on.
She doubles as my spine
when the one inside
of me calls in sick.
She smiles the way
envelopes do when
they swallow good news
and her laughter sounds
like God practicing the clarinet.

She's the most
amazing person I know.

I want to marry a
woman like my mother.
I will accept her in
whatever color she arrives in.

A Lot Like You

I was told
the average girl begins
to plan her wedding
 at the age of 7.
She picks the colors
and the cake first.

By the age of 10,
she knows time
and location.

By 17,
she's already chosen a gown
and a maid of honor.

By 22,
She's waiting for a man
who won't break out in
hives when he hears
the word "commitment."
Someone who doesn't
smell like a Band-Aid
drenched in lonely.

Someone who is more than
a temporary solution to the
empty side of the bed.
Someone who'll hold her hand
like it's the only one he's ever seen.

To be honest,
I don't know what kind
of tuxedo I'll be wearing.
I have no clue what my
wedding will look like.

But I imagine,
the woman who pins
my last name to hers
will butterfly down
the aisle like a 5 foot promise.

I imagine,
Her smile will be so large,
you'll see it on Google maps
and know exactly where
our wedding is being held.

The woman I plan to marry
will have champagne in her walk
and I will get drunk on her footsteps.

When the pastor asks
if I take this woman to be my wife
I will say yes before
he finishes the sentence.
I'll apologize later for being impolite,
but I will also explain to him
that our first kiss happened 6 years ago
and I've been practicing my "Yes"
for past 2,165 days.

When people ask me
about my wedding,

I never really
know what to say,
but when they ask me
about my future wife,
I always tell them,
her eyes are the only
Christmas lights that deserve
to be seen all year-long.

I say,
She thinks too much,
misses her father,
loves to laugh
and she's terrible at lying
because her face never
figured out how to do it correctly.

I tell them,
if my alarm clock
sounded like her voice,
my snooze button
would collect dust.

I tell them,
if she came in a bottle,
I would drink her
until my vision is blurry
and my friends take away my keys.

If she was a book,
I would memorize
her table of contents.
I would read her cover-to-cover,
hoping to find typos
just so we can both

have a few things to work on
because aren't we all unfinished?
Don't we all need a little editing?
Aren't we all waiting
to be read by someone,
praying they will tell us
that we make sense?

She don't always make sense,
but her imperfections
are the things I love about her the most

I don't know when I will be married.
I don't know where I will be married,
but I do know this

Whenever I'm asked
To describe my future wife,
I do so as best as I can
and every single time

…She's sounds a lot like you.

Turning Tables

You are a sentence
with no punctuation.
A kaleidoscope of colors
I don't remember
learning in elementary school.

Your voice is a sound
I've been looking
for my entire life.

Your face is the only sunrise
worth setting my alarm clock
early enough to see.
If I could
I would shape shift into the
first thing you think
about in the morning
just to make sure
I wake up next to you.

I love u in a language
that I don't fully understand.
In words I haven't hoarded
enough courage to forklift
out of my chest.
I hear that karma is vengeful
and also a light sleeper
so I've chosen to love you like this.
Quietly.

I'll call your phone
and hang up before

it actually rings
write you poems
that you will never read
and when I see you in public
I'll stick my hand inside
a bag full of things
I haven't done since you left
and pull out a smile.

I'll say something like,
"Hello…it's nice to see you"
and keep walking.

How to look like a stalker

Pick someone interesting.
Have a conversation with them.
Start off the dialogue
by assuring the subject
that you are not a stalker.
Do so by saying something like,
"I'm not a stalker"
"I'm not really a stalker"
"Do you think I'm a stalker?"
Or
"Does this make me
sound like a stalker?"
Because whenever you
mention the word "stalker"
it automatically makes
you look like a stalker

Follow them on twitter,
re-tweet everything they say.
Add them on Facebook,
like all of their pictures,
statuses,
and poke them.
Constantly.

Get their phone number.
Preferably not from them.
Send them pictures…
of you,
…in a wedding dress.
Let the caption read
"Hey babe, thinking about you."

Call 4 times
a day.
Leave 3 voicemails
a day.
Make sure the 3rd one
is passive aggressive,
sound irritated,
like all of this is a
big inconvenience to you.
Try to make the subject
feel as guilty as possibly.
If that doesn't work,
get angry,
cuss them out.
Then call back,
apologize for overreacting.
If the subject still doesn't respond
call from a blocked number.
If they don't pick up
leave another voicemail,
cuss them out again.

That'll show them.

My Honest Poem

I was born on July 27th.
I hear that makes me a Leo.
I have no idea what that means.

I'm 5'6 and a half,
I weigh a hundred
and forty-five pounds,
I don't know how to swim,
and I'm a sucker for a girl
with a nice smile
and clean sneakers.

I'm still learning how to whisper
I'm loud in places
where I should be quiet,
I'm quiet in places
where I should be loud,
I was born feet first
and I've been
backwards ever since.

I like ginger ale,
a lot.

I've been told I give
really bad hugs.
People say it feels
like I'm trying to escape.
Sometimes, it's because I am.
I get really nervous every time
someone gets close enough
to hear me breathe.

I have an odd fascination
with sand castles and ice sculptures
I assume it's because I usually
find myself dedicating time to things
that will only last a few moments.

That's also why I fall in love
with women who will
never love me back.
I know it sounds crazy,
but it's actually much
easier than it seems
and I think it's safer that way.

Relationships remind me
that I'm not afraid of heights
or falling,
but I'm scared to death
of what's going to happen
when my body hits the ground.

I'm clumsy.
Yesterday I tripped
over my self-esteem,
landed on my pride
and it shattered like
an iPhone with a broken face.
Now I can't even tell whose
trying to give me a compliment.

Sometimes,
I wonder what my bed sheets s
ay about me when I'm not around.
I wonder what the curtains would do
if they found out about all the things

I've done behind their backs.
I've got a hamper
full of really loud mistakes
and a graveyard in my closet.
I'm afraid if I let you see my skeletons,
you'll grind the bones into powder
and get high on my fault lines.

I've never been in the military,
but somehow I ended up with a purple heart
I think I got it from beating myself up
over things I can't fix.

Some days, I forget
my skin is not a panic room.

Hi,
My name is Rudy.
I enjoy frozen yogurt,
people watching
and laughing for
absolutely no reason
But I don't allow myself
to cry as often as I need to.

I have solar-powered confidence
and a battery operated smile

My hobbies include
editing my life story,
hiding behind metaphors
And trying to convince
my shadow that I'm
someone worth following.

I don't know much,
but I do know this,
Heaven is full of music
and God listens to my
heartbeat on his iPod.

It reminds him
that we still got work to do

Tuesday

Today,
while walking,
I stumbled into the realization
that this body is a no bomb shelter.
It's more like a straw house,
a pile of sticks making
collect calls to the wind
wondering when it
will be picked up.

 I've spent my entire
life trying to be myself
and some days I'm
not sure who that is.
The last time I heard
my voice,
it didn't even sound familiar

Yesterday,
I saw my reflection.
It wouldn't look me in the eye
because he's too ashamed
of all the things
he will never be.

Sometimes,
there is a "help me"
chained to the ankle
of an "I'm doing alright"

Every day,
I try to fit this anorexic ego

into the costume of a confident man,
but fake smiles irritate my skin
and right now I have a
rash the size of confession

I'm a zip lock bag
full of apologies
I haven't found
the courage to give
to all the people
who deserve them.

When I'm depressed,
I'm willing to chase anything
that has no ambition of staying,
women and parking spaces
begin to look identical
and I treat intimacy like a fire escape
forgetting eventually
we both have to go home.

When you are lonely for this long,
you stop calling it lonely.
You call it Tuesday

Poem for Ashley

My friend Ashley
smiles like a pipe bomb full of fireflies.
Last month she got married.
The groom was a 26 year-old boy
with a short temper, no plans
and a heart like a Rubik's cube.
These days, her only hobby
is trying to find the combination
to his unconditional love,
but she can only figure out the colors
that match wounds he has left on her body.

He treats her like a small country
with no military and lots of oil.
He occupies her when he wants,
invades her borders,
depletes her resources,
I'm surprised Dick Cheney's face
isn't engraved on the back
of her wedding ring.

While watching CNN,
I came to the conclusion
that Ashley and Iraq
actually have a lot in common.
They were both attacked without reason,
blamed for things they haven't done
and both have no
weapons of mass destruction.

She is caterpillar that
has already turned into a butterfly,

but hasn't realized she can
spread her wings and leave.
Hasn't realized a relationship
between a unicorn and a dragon
is destined for failure.
I fear she will have to read
her bruises like instructions.

The first time he put his hands on her,
she came to my door with leopard spots
and I watched her tears fall faster
than the value of an American dollar.
She collapsed in my arms
and I held her like a crumbling city.

That day, she pulled her
planet from the solar system,
placed it in the center of my hands,
hoping I could make
her world beautiful again.

I knew what she wanted to ask.
Instead of offering her
a fruit basket full of advice,
I put her eyes on backwards
so she could look inside
herself to find the answer.

If I could,
I would've pulled the
question marks out of her spine
and used them to
strangle her insecurities.

But we were candles

melting down to our wicks
and I inhaled the smoke
from her burning soul
like her spirit was
made of nicotine.
I took her emotions
and tied them around my arm
until there was bumper to bumper
traffic in my veins.

I swallowed her story.
She made me promise to keep it
within the confines of my stomach,
but now, I am shoving this poem
down the avenues of my throat
and throwing up her secrets.

Ashley,
if you can hear this,
I'm sorry,
but the silence is killing me.
I'm afraid
it will do the same to you.

Monster

One day,
A little girl asked me
if I believed in monsters.
I smiled,
I grabbed the truth by its collar,
I wrestled it to the ground,
tucked it underneath my arm
and said,
"You know monsters aren't real."

At times like this,
I wish my sentences came with receipts
so I could take back my words.
I wasn't being completely honest.

When I spoke to her,
I almost choked on a secret
that has been stapled
to the inside of my throat
for longer than I can remember.
Not only do I believe in monsters,
but I've seen them whisper
themselves into existence.

I heard they carve nightmares
into the eyelids of the innocent
and linger in dark corner preying
on the unsuspecting.
Somehow, they've figured
out how to crawl through
8 millimeter film and
walk backwards into the dreams

of those who've never
been afraid to sleep.
I believe in monster
the same way I
believe in oxygen.

So how big is your closet?
How much space is underneath
the beds you shake
in the middle of the night?
You're a vampire.
A werewolf in sheep's clothing,
You swallow halos
and spit out nooses.
How can I not believe in monsters
when I see men like you,
walking with your knuckles
scraping against the concrete?

You stand, perched on the screams
of assaulted women
and squeeze into costumes
that fool the public into
thinking you're human.
How dare you have the
audacity to impersonate me?

How dare you pretend
as though there isn't a woman out there
scrubbing the inside of her thighs
until they turn stop sign red
trying to erase your
fingerprints from her skin?

How dare you believe your blood

is just as blue as mine?
When you speak
I can smell Dante's Inferno
on your breath.

I've spent the last 3 months
trying to figure out
how you escaped from hell
and wasted too many nights
thinking of painful
ways I can send you back.

I carved galaxies in
the back of my throat
just make your world
easier for me to swallow,
but I can't stand
the taste of your behavior.

Every time you cross my path,
I get the urge to tie you to a chair,
cover you in gasoline
and set your body on fire.

I am no Van Helsing,
but I've seen enough horror movies
to know how to get rid of you.

But I know even if I killed you,
there are still millions of monsters out there
pretending to be men.

For Troy Davis

It breaks my heart to say this,
but there will be no parade for you.
No holiday,
no stamp with your
face tattooed on its skin.
Your funeral
will not be on T.V.

Your burial will be silent.
The day will be cloudy.
Your family will cry an ocean
that we'll never know you
well enough to swim inside of.

Next year,
classes will not be
canceled on your birthday.
Half of us have already
forgotten your story.

It's what we do in America.
We forget things.

When they decided
to nail a 24-hour notice
to the front door of your body,
my stomach felt like a vehicle
that had no idea where it was going,
it turned so many times
I thought I would
vomit 50 stars and 13 stripes.

My heart was a tractor,
driving during an earthquake.
It was shaky and felt like it
might stop working at any moment.

I wanted to do something,
but I couldn't get my
hands to stop trembling.
I wanted to say something,
but my voice was a sledgehammer
with an amputated handle,
heavy and useless
I wanted to cry.

So I did.

To the Graduating Class of UC San Diego

Someday,
you will throw a penny
inside a wishing well.
It'll choke
because your dreams
are just too big
for it to swallow.

When the wind
disagrees with your voice.
When the walls laugh.
When the trees make jokes.
When the floor
questions your footsteps,
know, the truth is a drum machine
inside a house that
was built behind your ribs.
Your heart is an ocean of possibility
and it beats like a song called
"Right Here, Right Now."
Take ownership of your choices
because sometimes,
that's all we have left.

I dare you to be
more than a paycheck.
More than the echo
of textbook pages
blowing in the wind.
More than a desk
in a crowded room.
More than a Xerox copy

of an article you didn't want to read
for a class you never wanted to take.
I dare you to be more
than a Scantron waiting for answers

Be the pen that writes our history.
Be the ink that refuses to be erased.

And when the world
stands in front of you,
all daunting and scary.
I want you to stare into its eyes
And say
"I've been waiting for you,"
"I'm ready."
 And say it like you mean it

Somewhere, there is a cape
and a pair of spandex
with your name it.
This world needs a hero like you

Made in the USA
Coppell, TX
18 February 2020